Handshake With the Divine

Stories
Messages
and
Poetry

Handshake With the Divine

Stories, Messages and Poetry

Some of the poems in this collection first appeared in: We Are One, Follow the White Rabbit, We Are Forever, Come to Mount Shasta, We Are Light and Finding Our Way Home chapbooks; and on facebook.

Cover credit goes to Grandmother Raven, 2023.

Cover design by Catherine Preus, 2023.

First edition.

Published by Alexander Agency Books, Mount Shasta, California 96067

ISBN 979-8-9897287-0-1

Handshake With the Divine

Cheryl Lunar Wind and Friends

Preface

Handshake with the Divine takes the reader to new levels. How? By sharing some of the different ways we connect with the Divine as experienced by the author and the other contributors in this handbook.

How do you connect with the Divine?

Some methods illustrated within these pages are: prayer, breath work, the natural world, by creating through music, art and literature, allowing and releasing and by the setting of a specific intention.

I would like to express gratitude to the many friends who contributed to this collection.

I pray that...
My eyes see goodness in all people and all things. I feel love toward every living creature and gratitude in my heart. My positive attitude is infectious, even contagious. My smile brings joy to all around me. This spirit fills the hearts of others.

I pray that...
My words and actions are kind. Compassion is at the core of all I do. Seeds of forgiveness find fertile ground upon which to flower. My generosity touches those next to me and those I may never meet. Patience prevails.

I pray that...
I Am blessed with absolute clarity of mind and precious purpose. The fuel of passion burns ever so brightly in all my speech. Courage and caution are in perfect balance in my life. Humility becomes the foundation of my every accomplishment. When I ask, I receive the inspiration that is duly mine.

I pray that...
The breezes of peace and serenity fill my sails on this journey. The light that is me burns as a bright beacon to illuminate all that is right. My heart and hands are busy building a better world.
                              ----unknown author

The Alchemy of Love ~

Rumi

You come to us
from another world

From beyond the stars
and void of space.
Transcendent, Pure,
Of unimaginable beauty,
Bringing with you
the essence of love

You transform all
who are touched by you.
Mundane concerns,
troubles, and sorrows
dissolve in your presence,
Bringing joy
to ruler and ruled
To peasant and king

You bewilder us
with your grace.
All evils
transform into
goodness.

You are the master alchemist.

You light the fire of love
in earth and sky
in heart and soul
of every being.

Through your love
existence and nonexistence merge.
All opposites unite.
All that is profane
becomes sacred again.

Contents

Flame of Life
by Cheryl

Spark the divine in you--
Be the Divine Spark.

Much is said about love and fear being
polar opposites. To really step out of
fear, we need courage. Therefore, I say
courage is the opposite of fear.

In the Wizard of Oz, Dorthy's friends
were seeking;

The Tin Man- a heart/love
The Scarecrow- a brain/wisdom
The Lion- courage/power

These 3 sparks of life make up the 3-Fold heart flame.
Love, Wisdom & Power.

The Flame of Life.

Light Grind Don't Stop
by Cheryl

One step at a time.

The Divine Handshake is a fire in my heart--
burns,

Flames of love--
determination, knowing, confidence.

Omnipotence---
taking over all thought and feeling.

Bits and Pieces *(Five poems)*
by Maria Lodes

World as we know it
       ---an ongoing dream
Ephemeral beauty
       ---symbol of What Is...

Bits and Pieces
       weave my persona---
An outer garment
       woven from shreds...

Scraps from childhood
       ---past lives
Give color to the weave
       ---who i think i am...

Let it all go
       ---whatever you thought
Unless you do
       struggle continues...

Mending my image
       misses the point---
I never was
       who I thought...

Come away from the window
       ---stop staring outside
Seeing Within
       all things revealed...

Silence of the mind
       releases a trapdoor---
Passage to the Heart
       ---Awareness I Am...

Threads by Cheryl

Aloha...Akua
Aloha...Akua

I will hold the line.
Be an anchor.

I Am holding hands
with the Divine.

---A lifeline has formed.

Grab on the kite string
don't let it fly away!

Be the golden thread---
The thread of change
Evolution

Slip thru
the eye of the needle.

We are One
of the many threads
in this tapestry of life.

Open Up to Grace

by Omanassa Star

The breaking carried it all away,
All that was cherished and gathered
through the years--

Taking Indecision away,
Making room for newness--
for tears to flow,
that had been stacked away for years,
for screams to be released,
for numbed out pain to be felt,
for love to be shared,
caring to be alive again.

No matter how great the loss,
She found the allowing is greater--

Once we allow the heart to break,
and
Open Up to Grace.

Tears

by Cheryl

Tears
Open our minds---
Crack the shell of our consciousness.

I Am vulnerable---
because I Am free to be me.

My strength comes from my weakness.

My pain makes me beautiful---

An innocent's tears are more powerful
than
a warrior's sword.

Adventurer

by Mercy (Hawkwomyn)

And ~
Then there is flow
Where I Know
I'm fully protected
but not impeded
by rigidly set
parameters,
following inner
navigational fields ~
for Truth be known
I am an adventurer
who often sets sail
into uncharted domains

~ ~ ~

I develop
Substantiated
Trust to
Fuel my ship
Upon High Waters
Voyaging through
Seas rife with strife
~

Hawk's Perspective

by Mercy (Hawkwomyn)

Shut
behind walls
the Essence of Life
is obscured

Give me a Tree
a Mountain
a flower
drenched in dew

Penetrate my perspective
with a Hawk's point of view
swoop down for discovery
relinquish the role
saturate with honesty
I Know when I'm Whole

When I feel the sunrise
like a kiss to my soul
when twilight reminds me
to soften the goal

In embrace of
a pure mountain stream
a river resounding with
all of my dreams
for living a life
elegant & raw
close to the Earth
or nothing at all.

When the going gets tough, **Keep Going**

by Cheryl

I Am--
"Running up that hill"

Keep going. Know your way.
(Keep on keeping on)

Be firm, kind and bold.

Hopeful--

Hope opens the door!

Do your best--
Accept your role
as a creator!

Create ANew Reality.

I AM So Grateful

by Ray El

I AM Grateful! I AM Grateful! I AM Grateful!
For All God's Gifts to me.
I AM Grateful! I AM Grateful! I AM Grateful!
For All the things I see.

I AM Grateful, Grateful, Grateful,
I always have enough.
I AM Grateful, Grateful, Grateful,
To God I send my Love.

I AM Grateful, I AM Glad,
Always happy, never sad.
All Good comes to me,
My household and my life.
I AM Blessed beyond measure,
I'm so Grateful for my wife.

I AM Grateful for the Sun,
The mountains, rain and breeze.
I AM Grateful for the trees,
The flowers, birds and bees.
I AM Grateful for our car,
It takes us near and far.

I AM Grateful for our neighbors,
Everyone's so kind.
I AM Grateful for our home
It truly was a find.

I AM Grateful every day I have
To love, to laugh, to play.
Each night I give my Thanks to God,
I always like to pray,
Not only for myself – but for everyone on Earth.
May Angels fill each heart with Love
And bring forth God-rebirth.

May you, Dear Hearts, be filled with joy,
With Peace, Happiness, too.
Please know that God is Love,
And gives It all to you!

Boundaries

by Le'Vell Zimmerman

Setting boundaries is an expression of Self Love.

You are here to serve all, however it's through trusting your intuition that you know your own temporary limits at present.

You can trust that your supply will expand as you serve and expand your capacity of responsibilities.

Such an acknowledgment is a part of your development in maturity as a Leader of the New Earth.

YOLO (you only live once)

by Cheryl

Ever been to YOLO?
I drove past once---

Got me thinking.
What's next?
Am I missing something?

Is there something left to do?
Did I accomplish, what I'm supposed to?
What I signed up to do?

Can I be done?
Is it enough?

Create

by Le'Vell Zimmerman

Everything you do "matters".

Truly mature souls are never dependent on validation amongst this holographic illusion.

As you create "for you", you naturally inspire others.

This is about expressing yourself, where this is your core purpose of being alive in a physical body, beloved.

Seeking approval has always been a form of psychological enslavement.

As an expression of the Creator you are here to create.

This is not only the primary source of your increasing frequency, but also where you are healing the emotional distortions and blockages within your energy centers.

You are here to create the New Earth through your expressions beloved.

Creativity is God's function.

#333

Teamwork

by Le'Vell Zimmerman

Trusting yourself is a priceless gift of honor
that expands with cultivation of your
spiritual maturity beloved.

The silent acceptance of your own presence
is the key to the great secrets you are here to
share with all life here in the physical.

Only you can decide to reveal such a knowing
as an aspect of your journey here.

We will always support you, but we can not do
it for you beloved.

The prime directive and gift of Free Will can not
be violated.

We can only support you on your mission to the
degree in which you are open to such teamwork
in who we are of your Angelic Guardians.

#3333

Free Will vs Ownership

by Cheryl

In the language I was raised with, English---
things are described as in relation to belonging.

This, that----yours, mine.

Very young children are taught---
rights of ownership.

Relationships--
familial and romantic are described this way--
my children, my husband, my partner
My, My, My

Society demands payment for necessities;
such as homes, cars, food, clothes--

Is it any wonder, with receipt in hand,
we say---
my car, my snack, my apartment, my room?

Pets--
my cat, my dog.
Ownership.

My space, my time--leave me alone.

The prophet Gibran states--
'we do not own our children,
they are like arrows shooting
out to space'.

Is this why we are here? to collect
and own as much as possible?

Birds, trees and the earth
give their gifts freely--

Feathers, eggs, leaves, nuts, wood,
rocks, sand, water, ponds, creeks, oceans---

Giving is a gift of free will.

We can give of our time, energy,
compassion, patience and understanding.

The more we give, the more it grows.

The matrix teaches scarcity--
by holding back--
what is rightly for all.

Lets give freely---
Break the program---
Change the language of your thoughts;
and your actions will speak freely---

Giving, Loving and Allowing

Wish Me Well by Cody Ray

Make to take
Make to give
Which way is great
One way to live
Shivering in the cold
Rather than fit the mold
Creators need nothing stole
Straight line me to Divine
It's never too late
The road to healing is not straight!
Let it simmer a while
Don't let it boil over
I'm the lucky one
That's why I forgot to look down at the clover
May you always find the spring within
Drink from the infinite as the onlookers lights go dim
The closed loop system of hate will rot
The greatest teacher is one who can be taught
Fight the flow if you want to, it's your illusion
Use it as you will
It keeps on spilling
Spelling is the least of my troubles
Intentions by ten fold
Unravel new colors
There I am again
Original and alone
Better than being a king in house full of clones
Which way to midnight the hitchhiker asks
I say we just made it and poor him a glass
I miss her because I'm lonely
Of course I still got love for her
So tired of being unhealed,
Tend to the fire don't let it go out
It will overpower the sunrise
Like a whisper in a shout
Still it keeps me warm and I love the smell
Oh if they would listen
The stories I could tell
They are content out there chasing
The dog without a tail
Here's where I stop
Wish me well

Let there be light
by A'Marie B. Thomas-Brown

The Path of the Sun
The Way of the Son
Brilliance lighting up
The sky of my mind
The sky of our world
Spirited vespers
Of silent rays
Steams of vision
Cascade
Circling, delving, whispering
Landscape
Horizon in view
hanging hue
Remaining the same
Brilliance in full array
No matter the name
Love makes Its way
Upon the Day
As well as the Night
Paradigm flight
Let there be light

Be Your Prayer
by Alla Ren'ee Bogarth

...be awake to the life
that is loving you and
sing your prayer, laugh your prayer,
dance your prayer, run
and weep and sweat your prayer,
sleep your prayer, eat your prayer,
paint, sculpt, hammer and read your prayer,
sweep, dig, rake, drive, and hoe your prayer,
garden and farm and build and clean your prayer,
wash, iron, vacuum, sew, embroider and pickle your prayer,
compute, touch, bend and fold but never delete
or mutilate your prayer.

Learn and play your prayer,
work and rest your prayer,
fast and feast your prayer,
argue, talk, whisper, listen, and shout your prayer,
groan and moan and spit and sneeze your prayer,
swim and hunt and cook your prayer,
release and recover your prayer,
breathe your prayer,
Be your prayer.

Far Off Worlds
by Rita Chambers

We do come from
    far off worlds,
With joys, griefs
    and longings.
We are like prayers
    in search
of the one who prays.

What is a prayer?
by Cheryl

What is a prayer?

Prayers match
the occasion, person,
mood or need.

A prayer is an extension of self---
thoughts and feelings
put into words---

Spoken into reality.

An affirmation--
calling in a higher power.

A releasing--
Letting go--
Let go and Let God--
a giving of burdens
over to someone or something else.

In 'Science of the Mind'
prayer is called a treatment--
words are arranged in a
specific way--
the speaker has a belief--
an energy of confidence--
a knowing.
It is called Faith.

An agreement made
before this lifetime--
Renewed
by
ritual.

We are strengthened--
thru the ritual of prayer.
Dove like,
Peace Returns.

20

In the garden of peace
circle of Aspen
cathedral.

There
you can talk to Saint Francis, Mother Mary and the Budha
in the same day
Or
you can pray
to a different
Saint each day of the week.

I pray
when
my head
hits the pillow.

In communion--
thru out
the night.
My family of angels
with me.
Comforting, Consoling, Directing.

Messages
preserved
with ink on page.

I am ready
to dive
back in the pool.

Good nite.

The Blue Expanse
by Darrel Johannes

From end to end, with the ends ever expanding.
The nature of heaven itself being one of never
ending expansion.

'And of the increase of his kingdom there shall
be no end.'

The fullness being in a way an absence of all
clutter, and things of falsehood, of no real value.

Beyond explanation, the fact being, the beauty
of it and also that it is removed from human
language puts it in a place, where it cannot
be touched by the impurity and limits of our
plane of consciousness.

The yearning for the blue expanse is joy itself.
The journey actually more vital than the destination.
Joy being in the movement towards the thing that
draws.

This blue expanse, one must leave the confines,
the limits of the present reality to experience it.
It does not exist with our logic or because of it,
it lives by a different set of precepts; Love over
judgment and hope over despair.

Its nature is one of momentum and grace, loving
what is and it is on track and on time. It exists for
no particular reason in the way we understand
purpose. It cares about all but will not be brought
down to our problems. It asks and would so love
for us to simply lift up our eyes to the horizon and
embrace the beauty of it. Feel it, and for just a
while, become,
into it.

My Place by Darrel Johannes

Expansion from limited earth drama to places of source in the
ethers, the cloud places where energies originate.

It will all drop off with such ease,
the small limited being I wrongly came to believe I am.

There is nothing to miss here when the scope of my essence,
my rightful place
in the theme of the universe is understood and loved.

There is nothing to miss about confusion,
limitation and error.

I will know
just as
I will be known.

My Prayer by Jennifer H.

My Wish

is for peace, love, balance,

freedom and unhindered healing for all;

the land, the water, the spirits,

all beings and people.

Thank-You

Haiku
by Kyle Preston Hutchinson

When will I find peace?
A meditative prayer
Instantaneous

Our combined stories
Roaming the world for answers
Fountain pen of youth

Mirroring the moon
I Am only just one man
We breathe in pure Light

A crystal raindrop
Drifting without attachment
Being the river

Live in this moment
For that's all it ever is
The blink of an eye

Downloading haiku...
The words truly write themselves
Elemental speech

The Vision by Wesley Buniger

The work I see before me is none other than a labor of love.
It involves helping others get in touch with themselves by
way of working with their hands. As a vision, it came to me
a year ago, shortly after moving to Mount Shasta. I entertained
the idea, but tried to lose it in other activities, but still the
feeling remained...

So here it is---
People continue to come to me saying they appreciate that which
I create, always, they are surprised at the diversity of what I
produce.

But, unable to understand how I do it. To me, it is my breath. I have
meditated by doing for so long, it has become a way of being. The
vision is to impart this ability to others so that they of their own
nature and at their own pace become aware of being completely
themselves. This is accomplished by awakening to one's own
intuition by the use of common sense. Common sense is the field
where spontaneity finds it spark. It is that place, where according
to ones own personal clarity, authenticity finds its source.

Some numerical thoughts...

by Cheryl

Even a broken clock
is right twice a day--
So, if I say my birthtime is
6:00am then there is a
one in sixty chance that is
Correct.
I'm willing to play the odds,
After all-
it is my life, and
I turn 60 this year so I'm
feeling lucky.

Born on 12/63-
6/6/6- 3
@ 6am---

12-21-1963 @6:00 am.
3-3-1963 @6
6 - 6 - 6

Enlightenment

I have come with the message--
It's time- Awaken!

1963-
10+9
19=1+9=10=1

A One Year

Begin New. New Beginning.
This year I turn 60.

666- A new beginning.
Shine Your Light--
Be an example for all.

Humanity Awakening--You and Me

Songpoem by Sananday

Humanity Awakening, What a beautiful sight to see
Humanity Awakening no more poor or poverty
No more have and have nots
No more killing, dying--
What for?

Humanity Awakening, No more war-mongering
Humanity Awakening, Live in peace and harmony
Healing all hurt, creating heaven--
Here on Earth!
Humanity Awakening
Its up to you and me--to be the change we want to see.

Humanity Awakening

Humanity Awakening, Right here this moment, Now
Humanity Awakening, For the good of everyone
Humanity Awakening, Doing all we can!

Celestial Light Beings- We Will Be!
All knowing, All seeing--
Humanity Awakening, You and Me
What a beautiful sight to see.

*"No more death, pain or sorrow. The former
things have passed away."*

Musings on 12/12

by Cheryl

Someone New? Yes!
New is always good.
An old friend too? Yes!

Something old and
Something new--
Just like a wedding.
Now we need--something
borrowed and something blue.
I will wear blue.

Last time,
We checked out your garden--
and the mosquitoes thought I
tasted good.

Now, we are closing out
the year on a powerful
portal day.

Also, closing a chapter in
my life. 60. An ending and
a beginning.

Like the Great Egret---
I have no regrets!

Oblivion

by Cody Ray Richardson

I cast the machete into the wall---
to sever the connection
that had impregnated me with negativity,
dissected me down to my
Oblivion.

From there I sat and stared at my severed head
as the octopus laughed and I laughed back at it
for I knew it was part of me.
That I used to be.
I will no longer be a part of this chapter, that was me.
Now, Being more of a man and more in love and loving of the
people around me.
Sharing of love rather than severing, shattering--
obliterating all contact.
Now I know.

I must live amongst everyone forever--
there is no leaving them.

And here askew in the ocean of my realization,
I realized,
looking back at myself
That I was the master and the captain
That there was no sea--
        there was no ship
        there was no monster
        all along
There was only me
Eternal and Forever

Bloom Out of Sadness

by Cody Ray Richardson

In a sea of changes.
Where uncertainty prevails.
Will we be the captain of discontentment?
Trying to dictate the outcome.
Abandoned and lost in the water spout illusion of the past.
Watching the endless production of disdain.
Playing out over and over in our mind.
Or will we awake in the only real time.
Open our heart to now.
Embrace our blessings.
Thank what we have.
See the ocean of possibilities for what they are.
Or keep having a tea party on a tossing ship.
A ship going in circles.
Party of mad man archetypes.
Fools convinced they've been fooled.
Cast aways from the grace of goodness.
Spinning their wheels in the mud of ungratefullness.
Or open to gratitude.
Realize the cycles of change are the greatest gifts.
Freedom of will has got us here.
So far from the shore of the life we so dearly crave.
Freedom of will will guide us back.
Hope is a sure fire compass.
I will put the wind back in my sails.
Circumstance is an opportunity for innovation.
The blues are not sung by the royal.
The real songs of soul.
Written only from the awareness of those tried by fire.
Forged in the cauldrons of experience.
Unique as the waves that throw their vessel about.
The balance of a tight rope walker.
Earned from the swing of uncertainty.
Trust that there is a much grander author.

The story you are in is bigger than your woes.
If you knew how wonderful you are.
You would be paralyzed with vanity.
Shine like a fire fly.
Dance in the dark.
Ride the cycle.
Arise to the dawn of your soul.
Sleep no more in the shadow of self torture.
Bloom in the sun the gift of the world.
For you are a flower of God.
Planted and nourished by the sacred elements.
Strengthened by the trials of time.
Dance in the wind of change.
You are the finest art of the ages.

Priority by Le'Vell Zimmerman

You are your own "top priority" beloved.

You can't truly assist and/or support others if there is no sense of stability on all levels within you.

No, self sacrifice is not what you are here to do, where this is not the best example to set for those you intend to assist in healing.

Once again, self love is the foundation of all Love in who you are as the foundation of this holographic experience.

#333

No Accidents by Le'vell Zimmerman

You can trust yourself in all that is unfolding beloved.

It won't "make sense", because Love is not logical.

Infinite Intelligence is beyond the limitations of logical comprehension.

Just know that all is serving you in being your own design throughout this healing process amidst your intent to "come home" to your true self.

There are no accidents here.

To trust yourself is to trust God.

#333

Tourists by Cheryl

Pluto, Neptune, Venus, New Moons, Eclipses...
What's your sign?
                    Really asking "Who are you?"
Stretch out of your comfort zone---
construction zone.
What are you building?

Leaving Earth station,
what is your next stop
on the Galactic Greyhound?
Do you have a daypass or
are you a frequent flier?

Is there ever a Final Destination?

Will you turn left at Saturn's rings or
head straight thru the Sun's portal?

Did you pack a lunch, travel pillow, a blanket?

Are you meeting up with a loved one,
in a neighboring galaxy?

Have you ever been on the Rainbow Subway
and bumped shoulders
with a Leprechaun?

Is your other vehicle a Merkaba?

Are you traveling alone,
or with a group?

We are all Tourists here.

TIME and SPACE---

Contracts we signed---
in this Holographic Universe.

---learn your lessons
---participate well,
     and then
---move on.

34

Souvenirs by Damien Balderrama

In birth and death,
in growth and decay,
in joy and pain,
the deepest truths are all the same.
We are temporary travelers
upon this physical plane.
The lessons we learn in the flesh
are our souls souvenirs.

Sojourn by A'Marie B. Thomas-Brown

The occasion of separation
Taking a breath
Riding in on the oxygen
Mother and Child
Once held with Breath
Now separated with the inhale
To be rejoined on the exhale
Only to see that
We remain as we are
Peace and War
Love and Hate
Dual states
That permeate beyond fragmentation
A lamentation
For what was seen
To be illusory
From its outset
I digress

For in this
Is the Oneness
Division serves this purpose
A returning
To being
Eyes seeing
Singular
Ears hearing
The sound
Reverberating through eons and ages
The Sages
Of another dimension
Wisdom saged through experience
And individually collective Remembrance
That stations us
Living being
Of Spirit and Truth and Light
Reflected in the stations of opposite
A conduit to our returning
A sojourn

The grass withers
The flower fades

The scales fall
A returning to All
A crawl
A step, A breath
And with no words left
I wept
At the innocence

Of it all

"I am Loving Aloneness" by Lauren Willow Fox

While I enjoy autonomy
I also enjoy sharing
While I love freedom
I also love caring
While I love independence
I also love interdependence

In my aloneness
I cry my heart out
And I comfort me
I play music loud and lovely
There's nobody judging me
When I'm silly and goofy
I laugh at me

The silence
It's golden
I live in a box
Walls, floor and ceiling
Sometimes the silence is so loud
I'm grateful for the drip in the kitchen sink

Is this why people become hermits?
God, am I on a path to love aloneness?
Now I make pancakes for myself on Sundays
Now I dance by myself in the living room
Now I watch movies alone
Now I cuddle with my electric blanket
Now I talk with myself in the mirror

I remember
So many of my smiles began with you
Just listening to you breathe
made me so happy
Now I listen to myself breathe
I contemplate my existence, my purpose, my joys

Am I loving aloneness?
I remember my time with you
And it makes me smile

Family makes me happy
I am loving aloneness
It's my mantra for awhile

God is showing me who i am
I am loving Aloneness
Like a tree in the forest
Like a bee in a hive
Like a flock of wild geese
Only the wise know that separation is an illusion

I am loving Aloneness
I am loving Al-one-ness
I am loving Al-one-ness!!!!
Do you want to come over for breakfast?

Many thanks to these contributors:

Omanassa Star

Maria Lodes

Mercy (Hawkwomyn) Talley

A' Marie B. Thomas-Brown

Ray El

Le'Vell Zimmerman

Cody Ray Richardson

Alla Re'nee Bogarth

Rita Chambers

Darrel Johannes

Jennifer H.

Sananday

Kyle Preston Hutchinson

Wesley Buniger

Damien Balderama

Lauren Willow Fox

Rumi

and the unknown author

Author page

Cheryl Lunar Wind lives in the Mount Shasta area in a little town called Weed. She is a practicer of Mayan cosmology, Lakota ceremony, Star Knowledge and the Universal Laws including the Law of One. Her hobbies are writing poetry, music, dance, drum circles and love for all life; plant, animal and crystal. Cheryl has been a guide and spiritual teacher for many years. Now she shares wisdom and wit through poetry, and has published poetry books; Know Your Way, We Are One, Follow the White Rabbit, Love Your Light, LIFE: Shared thru Poetry, Come to Mount Shasta: Sacred Path Poetry, We Are Light, Finding Our Way Home, and now Handshake With the Divine.

Testimonials---

www.ingramcontent.com/pod-product-compliance
Lightning Source LLC
Chambersburg PA
CBHW071740020426
42331CB00008B/2105